A Better Human Now

Insights from an Organ Transplant Survivor

Craig W. Huber

HUBER
BOOKS

Copyright © 2023 by Craig W. Huber

A Better Human Now

ISBN: 979-8-9854327-4-9 (eBook)

979-8-9854327-5-6 (Paperback)

979-8-2240911-3-3 (Paperback Dist.)

Contents

Dedication

To all my children and grandchildren, this book was written for you. When I was told that I was dying, all I could think about were all the things I should have told you. This book is the result of that soul searching. It isn't *everything* you'll ever need to know, and hopefully in my "extended stay" in life I have been able to communicate much more than what's inside this book. It is with all my heart that I want not only to tell you but also to show you with my own life as I work these truths out in front of you.

Hopefully, when I'm gone, on my last day I was a better human than the day before.

We as a family are a blended family and we came together by choice, not birth. I love you all more than you'll ever know! Please, never let a day go by again unintentionally. Live your life to the fullest and enjoy every moment whether in good times or times of trial.

Embracing the human experience,

Dad (AKA Craig, Bubba, Grandpa and someday Great Grandpa!)

Preface

My first book, *The Hero Within*, wasn't meant to be a memoir. I originally wrote it to share my experience with people who, like me, were facing an organ transplant. Thankfully, I was persuaded by my editor to make it a memoir—which in turn became a bestseller. It has stirred many hearts since it was born on a laptop perched on my lower abdomen while I lay in bed recovering.

It's with that same motivation that I hope to stir hearts again in *Better Human Now*. These are all things I've been working on since the day I awoke with a new organ and, even more importantly, a new chance on life. Let's begin this next journey together!

Chapter 1

The "Circling Dog"

At the beginning of producing the audio book for *The Hero Within*, I had a conversation with my long-time friend Jay (who would also narrate the book) about a strange dog that lived next door to him as he was raising his children.

Jay began the story saying that every time he and his boys were out in the yard when the neighbor was out, she would have her dog with her. Now before you say "big deal," hear me out.

She would walk through her yard and the dog would follow. Still no big deal. Then he told me that the dog always ran in a series of small circles to follow its master. The only way the dog could go forward was by spinning like it was chasing after its own tail. This little dog was spinning like a top everywhere it went.

So, after seeing this several times and being an inquisitive person, he asked her basically, "Why can't your dog just follow you instead of spinning?" Her answer shocked him and the boys. She replied that it was a rescue dog that she had adopted. The dog had been abused and kept in a cage all its life so whenever it got excited about getting to eat or whatever, it would spin in the cage. That is a very sad story! A perfectly good dog kept in a cage all its life is horrendous to say the least!

Then this kind lady got the dog and tried to introduce it to the good life, a life of love and pleasure, but all the dog could do was spin. It had been in the cage so long that it had forgotten its days as a puppy frolicking and being loved. Now no matter what, it just kept spinning. The poor dog had been so conditioned by the cage that it FORGOT how to live like a regular dog.

This really hit me hard. For one thing, no animal should ever be allowed to live a life like that! To say the least, it's. . .inhumane! Secondly and perhaps even worse was that on its own it couldn't break its life's habits that had been so deeply engrained.

As Jay was telling me the story, I realized that all of us have the possibility to become like that poor dog. Life has a way of caging you in and creating a new you that was never supposed to be. You weren't meant to spin your whole life; you were meant to frolic!

Every day is a choice: to conform to what the world is pressing in on you to keep you spinning or to get out of the cage as EARLY as you can! My cage broke open when my death sentence was given. It was then, and only then, that I realized I had been spinning for over fifty years! What will it take for you to get off the merry-go-round of life; to start really living and not just keep spinning?

Look at all the things people go through in life. Sometimes we might even watch someone's life fall apart and comment with, "You think they would have learned by now!" Often that's not the case because they just go back to spinning and keep getting caught up in *what they perceive as life!* When you're in the cage, that's all you know, and if you don't get out "early" enough you will spend the rest of your days exhaustively spinning.

The following chapters are NOT to tell you how to live your life! They are simply my take on what it means to break free from "just another day." These truly are things that I continue to strive toward. Truth grows within us; it doesn't come from the cage.

It's time for us to grow from the inside out together, freeing as many in the cage of life as possible as we also work things out for ourselves. On our journey through this life, let's remind ourselves of that dog and confirm that today is the day to quit spinning and finally walk out of the cage. C'mon, let's start. We've got some frolicking to do!

Chapter 2

Embracing Uncertainty

When you Google the word uncertainty, you'll see:

un·cer·tain·ty *noun* the state of being uncertain "times of uncertainty and danger" something that is uncertain or that causes one to feel uncertain. *plural noun*: **uncertainties** **"financial uncertainties"**

What is the best definition of uncertainty?

Uncertainty, doubt, dubiety, skepticism, suspicion, mistrust all mean **lack of sureness about someone or something**. Uncertainty may range from a falling short of certainty to an almost complete lack of conviction or knowledge especially about an outcome or result.

We have been trained from the beginning of our lives that things are certain. "Don't touch that, it will burn you!" we were told. Most of us battled certainty and touched it anyway. What happened? We certainly got burned!

We develop an idea in our heads that all things are certain. We plan a certain vacation. Flights booked is certain, reservations are certain, who you're traveling with is certain, the days you take off are certain, and your pets are certainly taken care of. You are on your way to a certain destination! Excitement unlimited is certainly just around the corner and you are certain that you need time away. You've been exhausted lately and can even smell the evening coastal air while you think of walking the beach.

Then out of nowhere uncertainty hits. Your traveling partner gets sick, a hurricane comes through your paradise, or perhaps you lost your job the week before. Hear me clearly when I say, "**Uncertainty happens!**" It is not a question *if* it will occur, it's a question of *when* it will occur.

In the years I spent as a pastor, I found people always asking things like, "Why does God allow good things to happen to bad people?" and its counterpart, "Why does God allow bad things to happen to good people?" First let me say just one thing. You are assuming that the people are good or bad and that your belief is a certainty. Haven't you ever seen on the news a neighbor that finds out that they lived next door to a horrendously evil person? The shocked neighbors usually say things like, "They always seemed pleasant enough. I don't understand how this could happen."

They were certain that they lived next to a good neighbor. You **don't** know what goes on behind closed doors. You don't have that ability! To immediately classify people as to whether they are worthy of a blessing or a curse is a human fault. We want to view most people most of the time with certainty. If we feel uncertain about someone, we are often given to rumors or suspicion.

Perception is reality

My dad was a custom home builder. In my teens I would ride with him through neighborhoods with some very expensive homes (some that he had built).

He told me one day, "Craiger, see all these houses?" "Yeah. . .so?" I responded in my typical teenage tone.

"Most of these homes are only partially filled with furniture, and it's all in the front rooms," he went on to say. Once again in my snotty teen voice I asked, "Okay. So?"

.   .   .

"Well, it's like this," he said. "They spent way over what they could afford to LOOK like they have money. Now they're in deep debt, but they think they look prosperous!" Then he said something that I still remember today. "People with real money (meaning big money) don't look like it." I think it was then that I started a fascination with people and why they do the things they do.

It was then that even though I thought I grew up in a wealthy area, I realized that some were just "players" in a game they couldn't afford. I had believed with all certainty that the whole subdivisions were filled with well-to-do people. Why had I believed that untruth? Why had I been certain about everyone who lived around me? I had made assumptions, or should I say, I went by outward appearances. This is where we get into problems, or as golfers say, "We get in the weeds." It's a tough spot to get out of.

I have said for years that "perception is reality!"

Have you ever thought about a person and wondered, "How did they ever get themselves in such a mess?" What was thought of as certain was found out to only be an assumption. We make wrong choices all the time, believing we've found certainty, when all along it was an assumption or opinion.

. . .

Not everything you believe is true! You change all the time due to your belief of what's certain. Sometimes the change is good and sometimes it's bad. **What you believe makes you who you are!** At least until uncertainty comes, and then it will destroy your belief pattern.

Here's an example from my own life. When I first met my wife Cindy, we somehow got in a conversation about organ transplants and whether I was listed as a donor. (I think we were getting drivers' licenses.) I told her emphatically that I didn't believe in organ donation. She asked me why. My only answer was, "Cause that's the way I believe! You're just not supposed to." I was certain about my answer, even though I had no truth to stand on. Worse yet, I used my faith to back it up (no evidence again). I believed in something that had no basis, but I was certain it was true.

When uncertainty arrives

Now if you read my other book *The Hero Within* you know that I'm an organ transplant survivor. That's my "inciting incident." It's even in the subtitle of this book! When uncertainty hit, it paralyzed me. How could something I believe in be so wrong? It's not enough to say you believe something with all certainty if you can't back it up with WHY you believe. Uncertainty will come your way, my friend, and it won't be pretty.

. . .

You can tell people all day long about how right you are about things by saying, "That's just what I believe." Yet that doesn't make it true, and to top it all off it's a statement of self-isolation. When people make these statements as a group, we call it church, government, or any faction that calls others to side with them over a certain belief. I can hear you yelling, "Well, what's wrong with that?" Nothing, except when you exclude or even hate people who don't "believe" like you!

The time will be probably be sooner than later that uncertainty will come and shake you to your foundation. It is then and only then that you will become willing to look at your own beliefs. It is then that you decide humbly what is really important and what is just a façade. Uncertainty will come and your world and life will be tested. It might be sunny today, but it will rain, and it rains on everyone sooner or later. "For He causes his sun to rise on the evil and the good and sends rain on **the righteous and the unrighteous**,"[1] is exactly how Jesus said it.

Let's go back to communities. We will talk in a later chapter about community and its importance. Whatever group you belong to, please make sure that its beliefs aren't made on certainties created in their own minds. Think how disappointing it is when one of our heroes comes up dirty or scandalous. We can't even imagine how someone so perfect could do such a thing. Why did it sting so much?

.   .   .

It's because we believed in a certainty that wasn't there. We didn't see it for what it was worth. We thought we knew them, but we only knew the façade. Yes, leaders fall; after all, they're human. How could we have forgotten? Often you only see what people want you to see, not what they are struggling with. This, my friend, is one of the reasons why we have such an upswing for mental health awareness. It's a hidden disease—sometimes even for those who are struggling with it.

What are your truths?

If you had told me three years ago that the world would shut down for over a year due to a virus, that I would unexpectantly become sick with last stage liver disease and have an organ transplant I didn't believe in, I would have considered you a nut! Or possibly even a lunatic trying to warn me of "bad days ahead." I would not have believed you.

I was certain of how things were. My perspective was my reality. Then uncertainty came—with all the tumultuous power of a category five hurricane—and washed away my foundations of belief that were built on nothing but my perception of what I *thought* was certainty.

What houses survive the biggest storms? The answer is the ones with a strong and true foundation. The ones that aren't built with bad, cheap, or even wrong material (perceptions) for their foundations usually don't fare well with larger storms. We need to question the foundation (premise) upon which we build before the storm.

I'm sure that for most of you it's a sunny season and I'm not trying to ruin your days of bliss. I'm just trying to get you to really see that you don't know the future! You just have a perception of how it will go. Everyone does. Yet it's more important to make sure your perception is in the now, not the future! Make sure that your foundation is solid. Mine was not, and it is tough dealing with uncertainty when you have built your life on a foundation of nothing but personal perception.

Before I started this book, I was discussing it with about five other authors in a small group setting. I told them that there were things I learned from "the inciting incident" and that I needed to get it out into the world. To my surprise no one was excited, no one even gave a "that's interesting" type of comment. Just quiet. Pin-dropping quiet.

So, I spoke up and said, "I have been working on these truths in my own life." Then everyone started speaking almost in chorus, and one author's voice stood out over them all to sum it up for all of them: "I don't want to read a book about you telling me how to live! We have enough of those. But when you said this is what you're learning and are trying to practice, that's a book I would read!"

. . .

She went on to say how she couldn't relate to me because she had never looked death in the face, never had a life-threatening disease. It woke me up to the importance of not just climbing on a soap box but also trying to lead people out of the cage of "just going through life" mode and helping them learn to accept uncertainty.

You only have right now and this moment. That's it. Simple and yet disturbing. Yesterday is gone, and you can't relive it. Tomorrow isn't promised. All you have is today. If it's going splendidly, enjoy it. Be in the moment. Live by the second!

Cindy (my spouse) almost lost her life from going septic before having a tumor removed and spending two weeks in the hospital. This was before I ever met her. She would always give me the bit about, "Enjoy today. . .you don't know if you have tomorrow." I tried to understand, but I believe I was (like so many of us) just trying to make it through another day.

I didn't know how to deal with uncertainty; I hadn't been told yet that I wasn't going to live. My foundation had never experienced even a low-category hurricane. It had only been through a few rain sprinkles with no problems. Little did I know that the foundation in my life was just about to take a beating from a storm I never saw coming.

Surviving the storms

Rarely do the storms of life come when we expect, and one experience almost showed me the reality of Cindy's "live in the moment" speech.

A business customer of mine who lives in my town was home one night with her husband. It was much like any other night. You know the drill, and you probably do it nightly. That night her husband decided to take the dog out for a walk. Nothing uncommon, he was just going through the motions of the day. It was probably just another day for them and even for the dog.

He put a leash on the dog and left for their walk. Minutes later she heard a funny noise at the door. She walked over to the front door and realized it was scratching that she had heard. Opening the door, she found the dog with the leash still on, but no husband. Confused, she stepped out of the house and saw police lights about half a block down her street. Her husband had been hit by a car on her 30-m.p.h. neighborhood street. A good day turned to a bad day, and in a moment multiple lives suddenly had to embrace uncertainty.

Think about all the lives this impacted: the driver and his family, all the victim's family, first responders, the list goes on and on. It hit me hard, and for a moment I embraced my own uncertainty. Then the next day came, and life happened, and I forgot about my uncertainty. I was like the circling dog and went back into my cage for a sense of comfort. Back to living for the weekend or the next vacation, forgetting Cindy's advice of living in the moment.

I don't care for fear mongers! Nor am I trying to be a downer. I am, however, the guy who loves life like never before! I am that person who was always positive in my outlook, but that didn't keep me in a mode to live every moment of my life to the fullest. Then I was told my days were running out! Then and only then life became important by the minute. I came to the realization that yesterday was gone and tomorrow might never come.

When people feel uncertainty, they inevitably point their finger at others. We tend to judge people on why they have problems. Like I said, even religious or political organizations fall into this habit. This was especially true during the pandemic, when the finger pointing grew wild from NOT dealing with uncertainty.

No one wanted to admit the uncertainty about the virus and its effect on humanity. So, suddenly everyone was an expert and started pointing at anyone who opposed them. It wasn't the opposing people or even the virus that was the problem. It was our lack of ability to deal with the uncertainty of what was next.

. . .

During the period of my non-stormy life, I'm sure I might have even made some snide remarks about why some people were in a personal storm. Now I realize that all of us will be rained on, and your foundation will be tested sooner or later.

I have also come to see that a lot of people I run into are wet or very wet from the storms of life. Ours is not to explain to them how they got into the storm or even how they could or should have done better. We are called to help them embrace uncertainty.

This wouldn't be easy without embracing the next lesson that I learned and have been practicing since my inciting incident.

Chapter 3

Empathy, Miracles, and Changing Internally

In the last book I stated that I had pastored and was in the ministry for a couple of decades. I studied and earned my ministerial license with two different denominations. Then I started a non-denominational congregation and was there for years.

With all that training and being around people of faith every day for twenty years, you would think the topic of empathy might have come up. Yet I have no memory of myself or anyone else teaching about this topic, probably due to its lack of popularity for those with and without faith. I might point out that ultra-religious people are often found to be without a lot of empathy, many times living a façade as we discussed in the previous chapter.

. . .

When I pastored it was during a time when two highly acclaimed televangelists were pointing fingers at each other and calling out each other's sins. When it all came out in the wash, they were each exposed for doing the very thing that they accused the other of doing. Somehow everyone forgot that these two were human and subject to uncertainty. Some of their fans or followers lost sight of their own faith over it. Frankly I'm over ultra-religious people.

That last statement just goes to show you that I need work too. This is an internal work, not external. Internally I need to even be more empathetic to those I don't agree with. Since the "inciting incident" I truly have cared about people in a deeper way. I'm definitely now way more empathetic toward my fellow humans. That's because something in me broke and looked like it couldn't be fixed. Empathy is completely different than pity or sympathy or even feeling bad for someone. Empathy holds out a hand and asks how it can help. Empathy is the birthplace of miracles.

Strengthening internal foundations

We don't wear empathy; we don't put it on like a positive smile or a frown of concern. It's a product of an internal work. Many people try to change from the outside in, but often this will lead to failure and frustration. Over recent years it has come out that addictions often come from our internal beliefs. Let's start with an easy example like dieting.

When we are truly empathetic, we quit pointing fingers and simply root for "team human." Dieting is often needed when you overeat. You or a doctor might put you on a diet; it doesn't matter. Yet, how is it that some lose weight on a diet while others do not? Scientist have recently been touting the mind body connection, and health and life coaches have popped up everywhere. Ever wonder why? Because they all say change starts internally! A lot of times the overeating is caused by an internal belief or conflict, perhaps like anxiety, nervousness, or bad self-image. The list could go on and on. The bottom line is if you want to change, start looking inward.

I will speak on this from a personal standpoint. If you read my prior book, you already know that I'm a liver transplant recipient. This was caused by a lifestyle that was simply not conducive to life itself. I was overweight, eating anything that moved, and worse yet I took up the habit of daily and excessive drinking—all of which led to my liver saying see you later!

Many people have told me that they wanted to know more about how I changed. It started prior to surgery with a twelve-week relapse-prevention program that my transplant team told me that I had to do. Really, at first, I was just going along, playing the game, and simply going through the motions. Then I had a realization, a revelation, a discovery of the writing on the wall. It wasn't necessarily what the counselor had said as much as I finally realized that **I needed to change!**

We've all been to the point when you get that "aha" moment of understanding. It usually comes with a "Why didn't I see that before?" With me it's been a series of those scenarios, one stacked on another. I started down the road of new self-discovery because I was finally open to it. I began trying to look at everything in my life because I almost lost it. I stopped drinking because I finally "had eyes to see" the truth of why I had picked up daily drinking.

People knew me as easy going and a fun person to hang around. It was a façade. Remember me talking about my dad's lecture? Outwardly everything was great until it wasn't. Internally there had been a war going on for years; externally I wanted everyone to see I was living a life that was great. My family first noticed the signs, then I finally noticed them: My internal war was beginning to manifest on the outside. It would ooze out occasionally where my loved ones would see it. They knew I was headed for disaster before even I did.

Where do we put all our focus? Do you remember? It's in the now, not back then, when we definitely decide to stop putting things off till tomorrow. It's in the now that I choose not to drink, and I don't consider myself as missing it. I've also lost a good seventy-five pounds and have successfully kept it off. How? Because I changed internally, not just externally.

Remember our talk about your foundation when the storms come? Your foundation is internal regardless of your faith, your political leanings, or even your social status. I changed when my beliefs changed, or you could say when I finally saw how things must first change internally. My drinking was from a lot of internal friction that I hadn't been dealing with.

I changed a lot internally, so much so that Cindy and I often refer to me as Craig Version 1.0 and Craig Version 2.0. If the truth was to be known and you have some knowledge of software, you know there are major and minor upgrades. The major upgrades change the number in front of the decimal while the secondary and consecutive changes are the numbers following the decimal.

So, you might be asking me, "Where are you now?" There have been so many minor upgrades and a few more major ones that I'm maybe at Version 2.34. I don't really know, as I haven't finished this book yet. I'm changing while I'm typing; reinforcing and enhancing my belief patterns. I am ever changing for the good or the bad, and so are you whether you're conscious of it or not!

Every journey is unique

Now some readers will question what the problem was inside of me that caused everything. It really doesn't matter, and you're missing the point! What is broke in me might not be broken in you. This is where people go off track because each of us is different and on a different journey.

Your mom was right, you are a special snowflake! So quit sitting and listening to and trying to be like the latest guru or public personality or even a friend. They are not you - period. You will run from one new thing to another trying to change from the outside in. (At least that's what a friend told me.) This vicious circle will continue until you stop trying to only change externally and instead work to change from the inside out.

Enough of me. Let's look at you, but not in a "here's what you need to do" way. Instead let me show you a new way to understand the real you. Disclaimer: I have and do use some scripture from the Bible, and I also often quote people from other religions. So, let's be fair about things and keep our finger-pointing at bay. I am for team human! I am a Christian and that's my faith, and I don't judge another's faith no matter what it is. If you look at my friends, you will see people of faith and people who are still trying to figure out just what they believe in.

. . .

It's true that some folks who are living externally are often pretentious and can also appear to be very religious, but with just fake fruit on the tree, per se, their façade will blow away sooner or later. They are way too busy to grow real fruit, and they use all their energy on judging externals rather than looking at their own internal needs. I'm working hard to not be that person. That said, let's get back to learning more about the real you.

Doing things simply to be seen by others is shallow and won't serve you well. My promise to you is this: If you change from the inside to the outside, you will be living a true life and you will turn into a light on a hill for others. That's why the whole New Testament was written. It is about Jesus trying to take a bunch of people who thought they were going to heaven from what they did externally and refocusing them into their internal world that needed a light shined on it. I know it's unpopular. It made a lot of people mad then, and it still does today.

As an ex-pastor (I like graduated pastor better), I truly believe we have done a real injustice by telling people how they must live externally yet never talking about their internal state. So, to try to undo some unhealthy things in myself and hopefully in you, dear reader, we will have to learn about ourselves and not others--even though that in itself is a tough job. But remember, I'm on team human so we can get through this together and grow some true fruit. One of the sweetest fruits is empathy, and it is the birthplace of miracles.

Nurturing growth

We've all grown some type of a plant before. If you say you haven't, then I guess you probably don't know about grass or even weeds. I personally can grow a weed like nobody's business! Let's take a look at the growing process. You plant a seed (or someone else does), then the plant, grass, weed, or whatever starts to grow. A child who gets really excited about this growing adventure might want to run outside and begin to pull on the plant to help it grow. Does it help? No, and if you take it too far, oops you just beheaded it! There is NO quick way to grow; it must happen naturally.

We know plants have three basic parts: roots (foundation), a stem or main part (that holds up everything), and branches with leaves or fruit to enjoy. Perhaps you might even grow enough fruit that others could come and enjoy it. That, my friend, explains the spiritual life no matter what faith or group you subscribe to. Even a scientist would back me up on this. The whole world understands some idea of this, but we just express or explain a lot of it in different terms. So, let's just keep it as simple as we can.

Back to the plant you almost beheaded--it is simply three functioning parts. I do know that it also contains millions of cells too, but for today we are only looking at the three major parts. You too are basically made up of three major functioning parts. (I'm not listing them in importance because they should all exist equally on the farm.)

First let's think about the roots. If the roots go bad, what happens? Next think about the stem. If the stem goes bad, what happens? If the leaves and fruit don't fully develop or if they fall off, what happens? If a part of your plant goes bad, you fix the bad part so the good parts flourish. It's Farming 101. When one of your three major parts go bad, the rest will generally follow.

So, what would you think about discussing *your* three parts? After all, this book is called *A Better Human Now*. What are your three parts as a human? Drum roll please . . . spirit, mind (or soul), and body. You've probably heard something like this before but maybe it was head, heart, and body or even maybe mental, spiritual, and physical. It really doesn't matter. They're man-made words trying to describe the three major areas in the human experience.

Remember, when any one of these parts is out of balance, sick, or crippled, it will affect the others. Just take a moment and think about times that you've experienced or even watched others experience situations where the mind affects the body or the body affects the mind. Throw the heart into the mix and you can tell why a lot of folks are walking around having their own internal personal civil war.

Let's define each part of ourselves so we know what to focus on. As a graduated pastor I saw a lot of people that had a real heart change, but their head was so screwed up it led to that civil war within themselves. Unfortunately, some lost the war because they were out of balance in their own triune parts.

The body

Since all three parts are equally important, let's start with the easiest part to explain: the body. Now I'm not a doctor nor have I played one on TV, but I have found my body more than once. You'll find it in an episode of "Oops, I hit the wrong nail with the hammer" game.

Some of you are more acquainted with your body than others. Maybe you could have gone through a medical ordeal like I did. That is when you really begin to have a healthy respect for it. I know my body and my transplant team also knows my body inside and out. I now can feel and tell things about my body that I never did before.

Case in point: During one post-surgery visit I complained about my shoulders aching. My doctor told me that I had probably been having symptoms for years but had never noticed it. I scoffed under my breath until I heard the next sentence when he said, "You probably never noticed it due to the drinking and then your illness."

You might be thinking right now about how I responded to that little piece of news. I had nothing to say but, "Huh..." He was probably right on his prognosis. I had practiced numbness with my body through the abuse of alcohol.

Please find yourself a good medical primary. Most men and really a lot of people don't go to the doctor "cause I'm not sick" is their belief. Let me ask you this. If you were going to add a second story on your house, wouldn't you want to first check the foundation to see if it could handle it?

If you're not going and getting a physical every year with blood work, your personal Taj Mahal could be being built on a foundation that you didn't even know was rotting. People typically just don't drop dead of heart disease, etc. Most of these things are treatable and all you need to do is allow an inspector (doctor) on your property to check out your foundation. I probably don't need to say any more so if you haven't yet, go find your body and treat it well.

Remember we are still going to talk about empathy, I promise! We are going through this to see where empathy comes from. You can look sad and concerned with your body in an attempt to show empathy. That would be very external of you, but that's not empathy.

The remaining two internal parts of us—mind (or soul) and spirit—are a little more difficult to pin down at first. So here goes a little more information about you and how we can become a better human.

The mind/head/soul

We'll start from the top with our next part which is the mind, and it is a little trickier to explain. Some of you will have already become mind ninjas while others, if they were being monitored, might be more "flatlined." For our studies it doesn't matter where you're at on your journey or what parts need fixing. All the upgraded versions of myself didn't fix problems in just one part of me. Different upgrades went into fixing various parts according to the needs at the time.

The head, the mind, your soul—all three of these are the same part, leaving only the heart/spirit, or the core of your being and your values, to cover. The words head and mind probably went down and assimilated inside your mind easy enough, although most of you probably had a tougher time with the word soul. This is because you likely consider the soul and spirit being the same. After all, doesn't your soul go to heaven? However, there is a difference.

· · ·

The word soul (found many times in the Bible) translates from the Greek word 'psychi' where we get our word psyche. Your soul allows you to know where you're at and translates that experience to you. It would seem to me that it would be important to know where you're at (or where you've been or even where you're going).

So, call it soul, psyche, mental, emotions, mind, or head, it's all the same part and often needs fixing. Truly, people can have a good body and heart and a screwy head/soul/mind. You could also likewise have your head and heart in the right place and your body out of alignment. Health and alignment of all three parts are what we want to strive for.

All three parts need to come into alignment with each other and flow as one. You are a three-part human, like it or not, so here's a doozy for you to think about. It is written in the scriptures that you were created in His image. For those of you who have studied that in more depth, you probably read something about that trinity thing. You know the Father, Son, and Holy Spirit being three separate divine entities and yet one God. I'm not trying to simplify God but if you're having problems understanding the trinity, simply look at yourself.

You were made in His image, and you are also three parts and yet you are one. Here is another way to explain triune things. Think of water. It comes out of your faucet into a glass. Or you could go to your freezer and get some ice cubes and put them in a glass. When they melt, what do you have? When you condense steam what do you get? They are all water, just three different forms. However, there is one major difference between you and God. He is the adult and you're His child, and we all know how children act up and get in trouble (some friend told me).

We will cover more on your mind in the next chapter.

The spirit/heart/core values

Next up: the heart, spirit, or core values. It is in your heart or spirit that true changes are made. We know already that all three parts of you need to be in alignment with each other, or you won't bear any fruit a.k.a. outward change. Religion for years has been frustrating people by **not** telling them they have three parts. I'm sure all of us have had that moment of "I really mean it; I want to change!" Probably there were some emotions involved, but you knew you meant business. Something changed inside. For me personally it seemed dramatic; for some it's a very somber moment; and for others it's just an inward decision.

You can have a squirrely head mentally and a body that's out of line and still have a good heart. I'm going to say something really hard now. If you have had a change in your heart, or perhaps in your faith, but then let the other two parts of you stagnate, you could be in trouble. Worse yet if you have a spiritual change and don't get your other three parts successfully upgraded.

Don't get discouraged when no one wants to sign up for that. What orange tree in a grove would you walk up to and think about eating its fruit? The one with a good trunk, leaves, and lovely oranges, right? What do you think the tree looks like if one of the parts are sick? Do you think you'd want that fruit? Simply put, be whole in spirit, soul, and body and people will be drawn to you.

Knock, knock. Who's there? It's me, empathy.

Empathy flows out of your heart, not your head nor your body. It is a deep sense that you have for others to a point where you would (if you could) exchange your life so they wouldn't have to suffer. This is why empathy is the birthplace of miracles. Empathy is not acting sad for someone or feeling sorry for them or even taking pity on them; it flows from your heart. This is why I say it's the birthplace for miracles. I think if you look and study, you'll find that everywhere you see a miracle you'll find empathy.

All those things like pity and being sad or sorry for someone are emotional and soulful acts, and that's a good thing for sure. However, let's instead allow empathy to come up from inside us and see what happens. Have you ever been told by a store clerk to have a nice day when clearly, they didn't mean it? Empathy causes you to mean what you say.

To be completely truthful, sometimes we all act a certain way around those who are suffering. It's the respectful thing to do, I suppose, but showing true empathy is always better.

Sometimes in my life I've even avoided those moments in others' lives when the storm hit them, purely because it made me very uncomfortable. I haven't always been the best family member, friend, coworker, or neighbor. Nothing can make up for that, but now I know I can be a better human to those in a storm.

Empathy vs. religiousness

When Jesus was on this earth He hung out with prostitutes, drunks, tax collectors, and all sorts of shifty characters. He didn't hang out with the externally perfect and very religious scribes, Pharisees, and Sadducees—and not because He didn't love them. They just refused and were indignant with rage toward Him because He was with the "unclean" people.

There is nothing worse than an enraged and indignant religious person. They will go through the ranks accusing everyone that's not like them because they believe that pointing out everyone's faults makes them look even holier.

One of greatest demonstrations of this is when they brought the adulteress to Jesus.

Basically, the story goes like this. Jesus goes to the Mount of Olives and goes into the temple area. He then sits down and begins to teach the crowd that had gathered. So far it seems like a really nice time. Then suddenly, the Scribes and Pharisees (the ultra-religious people of the day) storm in, disrupting everything. With them they are dragging a woman along and throw her into the center of the of the courtyard where Jesus was sitting and teaching. They are, like I said earlier, "enraged and indignant!" I mean they were really fuming!

Then pointing to the woman, they say, "Teacher, this woman has been caught in the very act of committing adultery. Now in the Law, Moses commanded us to stone such women; what then do You say?"[1] Now, outwardly religious people will debate scriptures with you all day long. Why? Because then they never have to take a good look at themselves inwardly. When you're a king outwardly, everyone else is your peasant and so it goes in the religious world.

Remember me telling you about those two televangelists pointing fingers at each other for the sin they themselves were committing? That's what was going on here in this story. The Scribes and Pharisees were outwardly holy and called all those around them to be the same.

. . .

This poor woman got caught. (I always wondered how. Were the accusers peeping?) She is thrown into the center of the courtyard waiting to be killed by stones. When people get hit by a stone, it's bloody. My boys proved this to me at a young age with each other. Now imagine being pummeled by many stones until you're an unrecognizable lump of bloody flesh. That's what the Scribes and Pharisees wanted and, while they were at it, they were going to discount Jesus' teachings by trying to trick him into answering incorrectly.

Now this is the part of the story when things get real, and I mean really straight-to-the-point real. Instead of answering their question, Jesus stoops over and begins to write in the sand with his finger. He then tells them, "He who is **without** sin among you, let him *be the* first to throw a stone at her." Then they all depart one by one.[2] The accusers already had everyone believing they were holy, so why did they suddenly all begin to dissipate? I don't believe Jesus was just doodling in the sand while trying to come up with a response. I think he was actually listing all the secret sins of the religious in the sand. They saw it and had nothing else to say.

He then asks the woman where her accusers are. She says she doesn't have any more. Jesus tells her that He doesn't condemn her either, and then tells her not only to stop but also not to do it again.[3] Take a moment and think about the characters in this scene. The outwardly religious were exposed, and the outwardly sinful and yet self-acknowledging woman gets a chance to straighten up and fly right. Well, that all went down backwards.

If you choose to see the "true you" inside, then you will walk with the knowledge that you aren't, nor will you ever be, perfect. It is then and only then you will move from an outward concern to providing true empathy that holds out a hand to everyone including the "unclean." You can do this! Just walk in the realization that you're human and while you probably don't have an answer for those in need, you can still show up with your empathy! That in itself gives people hope, and hope always comes before a miracle.

Internally you can grow as if a seed was planted in your heart from which will flow the essence of life to others. Everyone wants to eat from the orange tree that has good, luscious, and juicy oranges verses the tree with sick parts and little or no healthy fruit.

I have told you all this to explain the external and internal things to watch for. I can't ride on elevators in a medical building without asking people about their story. First, they are amazed a stranger even cares, and a lot of times all I can do is listen—or maybe even tell my story in hopes of encouraging them. Listening is always the first step. I've been amazed at how much empathy flows from me internally. I know this is not Craig Version 1.0; instead, this started happening when I got real with myself inside.

Yeah, the whole "you're going to die" definitely helped with me getting real with myself on all three levels. I know many of you have never been on death's doorstep with the doorbell having been rung, but you don't have to wait for that to happen in order to change. My greatest sadness today is how many years I lived not being in balance with my three parts, only worrying about the outer things that build status and comfort.

Empathy flows from respect

Today it is my mission to exhort and encourage people to be the best they can be by treating their fellow humans with the respect they deserve, whether "guilty" or not. I thank public servants all the time now; I just can't help it. I've made nurses cry because I asked them how they were doing, and I remembered to check back with them and see how things went. It means a lot to us when someone cares not only to ask but to also follow up with a call or email.

Empathy comes from within, and people can tell because it feels trusting to them. How about the waitress that evidently has an attitude today while she waited your table. Most would leave her a mocking tip and a snide remark on the receipt instead of tipping the courteous amount. Do you think she got changed and woke up due to your snotty remark and tip? My guess is she crumbled it up and cussed you, and frankly I don't blame her.

What about instead asking her "How's it going?" or saying something like, "You look like you're having a rough day," then listen to her reply. I mean truly listen, and please don't tell someone that "you know how they feel" if you haven't experienced their problem. That wouldn't be empathy now, would it? Maybe some people wouldn't suffer or even die from mental health if we were all on a mission of "kindness matters" and lived from our inside out. Here's a quick story about me thinking I had the empathy thing down—when I clearly needed more practice.

I was in the garage of a major hospital after an appointment that had gone well. I was happy and everything outwardly was good. I got in the car and started toward the departure gate. I saw there were two lines to two payment machines, and all the cars seemed to be making one line a lot longer than the other. I was then forced to get in the short line because the end of the other line trailed far around the corner.

So, there I am sitting in the short line watching a person keep repeating the same actions, with no success, on the machine that operates the gate. A couple of minutes passed—nothing; a couple more (seemed at least like ten) passed and still nothing. Meanwhile, the other line is releasing people out of the gate like it's a horse race. I try to get over and can't, then I look to the front of my line. That same car is still fooling with the machine. BOOM! I exploded with cuss words at the people in the accused car! Words came out that I normally try not to use. I was mad, vein-popping mad.

Then it hit me, again, that internally there were still things in me that needed work. Even though right before that I had talked to a woman in a wheelchair and had truly displayed empathy, under the pressure of having to wait I became a jerk. To make it worse, when the attendant came to help, I found that it was an older couple, and the wife was driving. I thought that if I caught a jerk like that yelling at my parents, I'd punch him square in the nose. I left the garage with more things needing change than when I entered.

Watch yourself. View yourself as others would. Do NOT view yourself the way you *think* they perceive you. Many times, we have a lopsided view of how people see us. If you think you need help with this, go find the most critical person you can, and they will help you see yourself differently. They typically have had a lot of practice and are good at what they do.

Please watch all of your three parts and make sure they're in alignment. Then above all please don't allow yourself to have your very own personal civil war. Protect your heart and soul while taking care of the one body that you were given.

. . .

Body: check.

Heart: check.

Head: oops...

In the next chapter we can talk about how I'm becoming a better human through a change to divergent thinking.

Chapter 4

Divergent Thinking

It seems to me that I process things best when I'm rested. Perhaps I settle down enough and focus best after I'm totally relaxed. Maybe it's then that I become like a blank chalk board ready for the next lesson. This is why I usually write in the morning or even after a nap. A peaceful me is a receptive me. Often, I will go lay down when I'm stressed and just center myself. When I say center, please don't go all meta-physical new age on me. It's just me taking a moment to get all three parts of me aligned.

I start with my body (usually first place where stress shows up), and I go through and consciously relax my body parts one at a time. I make sure my legs are relaxed, then the arms, then perhaps my shoulders and neck, releasing any tension I might have been carrying. If soothing music helps you, go for it. I almost always must have quiet, but that's just what works for me. Find what works best for you.

During this time, I mentally let go of things. Most things that we humans carry around in our minds aren't things we can change anyway. Some even would feel bad if they didn't worry. It's as if their worrying is keeping things (or perhaps even their world) together, but in fact it does nothing for us except harm. Being a worry wart and being careful are two completely different things.

After my body is relaxed and I have my thoughts under control, that's when for me internal things become clear. That's when I can pray and ask how I can change and be better. It's not please change Cindy or the kids (although I have prayed that before); it's more like here I am, what do I need to work on? Usually, I become so peaceful I'll doze off. Take that, insomnia! It was during one of these sessions at bedtime that I went to sleep and woke in the morning with the words "divergent thinking" coming up. I had no idea of what that exactly was, so I looked it up.

I Googled divergent thinking, and this is what I found. Merriam Webster defines it as: *creative thinking that may follow many lines of thought and tends to generate new and original solutions to problems.*

Without boring you with multiple definitions, it basically means to think on levels you're not prone to exploring. You are not only thinking outside of the box but also on different and less widely used levels with multiple views that you don't normally look at.

You probably came up with the same response I did initially: Huh...that's nice. Then I started noticing things and discovering perceptions that I never had before the inciting incident. With empathy I was able to see people on their level, not mine. So often we only see things our way! Worse yet we discredit anyone who doesn't think like us. No empathy there.

I started to understand that there are always at least two sides to every story. I just don't take things at face value anymore. Hey, that kind of fits in with us talking about facades and uncertainty. We talked about taking sides and pointing fingers. I didn't put you through all that for nothing. We are at this point on purpose and it's going to take everything we've been building on to understand divergent thinking.

The challenge of divergent thinking

Why is divergent thinking so difficult, you might ask. Do you remember being told as a kid that "practice makes perfect"? Well, it's actually correct, but let's look at that phrase divergently.

The phrase "practice makes perfect" also works in the negative realm, as in bad habits! What you practice, you will become good at! Start telling a few lies and it will eventually lead to more lies. Next thing you know you begin unknowingly practicing lying, and you become good at it! It can even get to the point that you begin to believe the lies yourself. Cindy and I both remember the times when all our kids "faked themselves out" while trying to cover their tracks.

I've seen adults justify their wrongdoing all the time by replaying a "justifying lie" over and over in their minds. How else could you do something that your heart is against? You allow it to play over and over in your mind until you override your heart and hurt yourself and the ones around you. You practice the lie again and again until you believe it. Many adults have ruined a good marriage because of this mental fault.

We are used to thinking only one way. Our way! After all, it's the only correct way, don't you think? If you don't believe me, think about the last argument you had. Why did you so fiercely defend your point? That's likely what caused the argument in the first place. Both you and whoever you were arguing with each 100 percent believed that the other person was wrong.

This is where divergent thinking comes in, since it basically allows you to see things in ways that you've never seen them before. You begin thinking on several levels rather than thinking on a single level (usually your own preconceived ideas).

Here is an example that I deal with all the time when I speak to people about being an organ transplant survivor. They typically say things like, "Well I'm glad you're all better now!" They tell me this usually from a place of caring. They came up with this from all the data they fed into their own personalized computer (their mind), and in their mind, you have a transplant and Boom! You're cured! However, all that is incorrect.

Having a transplant is a treatment, NOT a cure. People just haven't heard that. . .or perhaps folks do believe what they want. We often go through life with the wrong data or input that goes into our mind, creating our belief pattern. Have you ever heard about someone making a really bad choice? They made it on the data they had, and then it became their single view on the situation. Be diligent on what you fill your mind with, as it has become the modern battlefield in our lives.

Your mom might have also told you that "you are what you eat." All she really wanted to get across to you was that what you put in your body will cause an effect on your body. Hence, she told you to put the chocolate bar down and have an apple instead. She probably told you this out of love because she didn't want you growing up with health problems.

You're all grown up now and you get to decide what you put in your body! Good for you! On the other hand, some of us never disciplined ourselves and continue to choose the unhealthy habits as adults. Having a candy bar is so much easier than eating something good for you, plus all the cool kids are eating candy bars!

In North America we are especially given to trends which are often the reasons why we buy things. One example is fear of missing out (or FOMO). "All the other kids get to!" and "Why can't I have one?" were things you said growing up.

Now the power is in your hands, and you have control over your own life. You can eat anything you want, buy what you want, but why do you want these things? Because you were shown in a television advertisement or perhaps online that all the cool kids have one, so you run out—or more likely go online—and put yourself in "the gang" by buying the product. It's simple and effective marketing.

It goes even further than that. Many people are an open pit for a lot of junk knowledge. The media knows this, and so do marketers. I learned a lot while I recovered from my transplant, especially when I started taking classes on marketing. It's a scary thing to learn to be honest. I started seeing that basically we are taking in propaganda every day. I'm not talking about a political agenda (but that could also be true in some circumstances).

One of my favorite sites for synonyms gave these alternate words for propaganda: advertising, agitprop, brainwashing, disinformation, hype, information, newspeak, promotion, publicity, advertisement, advocacy, counter-information, indoctrination, spin, announcement, ballyhoo, boosterism, buildup, doctrine, evangelism, handout, hogwash, hoopla, implantation, inculcation, info, literature, marketing, misinformation, plugging, proselytism, publication, puffery, big lie, half-truths, party line and more. Did you notice that a lot of the synonyms for propaganda are negative influences like "half-truths," etc.?

Discovering your truth

Whether you want to believe it or not, other people have been shaping you to become the person they want you to be. Marketers don't care about you nearly as much as they care about you buying their product. I say this because there is a plethora of information and stimuli that you take in daily, both good and bad. This noise rattles around in your brain until you make some sense of it and develop an idea.

Think of it in this fashion. Your mind is a computer and data is being dumped into it daily from all these external sources. You process it and store the information for later use. Some topics you've been collecting for years often become the basis for your beliefs. I believed for all but two years (the last two) of my life that organ transplant was wrong.

Do you remember when I told Cindy that I didn't believe in organ donation? When asked why, my response was because that's the way I believe. BAD information was what I had consumed. Perhaps there are a lot of things that you believe but have never questioned yourself as to why you believe them.

As stated earlier, divergent thinking allows you to see things differently than the normal pattern. You begin thinking not only "outside the box" but on a different level, and this new way of thinking will cause you to reexamine some of your core beliefs. For some this can be unsettling and even disturbing, but remember this: Truth can withstand scrutinization! Falsehoods and propaganda cannot!

This is why many folks live for other people's approval or believe in things that they normally wouldn't because if "so and so" believes it, it must be good. We have gotten into a lazy habit of being an idea dumpster versus being a highly informed person who makes decisions based on wisdom, not just knowledge that we've collected. Soon you will be on your way to a healthier you by ingesting—and believing—only that which serves you.

This is why Mahatma Gandhi said, "I will not let anyone walk through my mind with their dirty feet." Garbage in, garbage out as the old adage goes. Put good and healthy things in and healthy stuff comes out. So, in a sense if you are not thinking healthy thoughts and share those ideas with others, it's potentially infectious. That, my friend, is propaganda, and it can be used for good and for bad. We all eventually spread our ideas. Let's start monitoring our mental diet and only infect others with good.

Practicing divergent thinking

How can we practice divergent thinking in our lives? Here are some simple and effective ways to help you grow your new outlook.

Brainstorming. This is a good place to start. When faced with a problem or challenge, try to generate as many ideas as possible, even if they seem unconventional or unrealistic. Don't worry about whether they're good or bad, just write them down or do a mind map if you're used to thinking like that. Just get everything down.

Question your assumptions. Challenge your preconceptions and look at things from several different perspectives. I recently read a book for authors by Becca Syme in which she talks about QTP, and if you've talked to me lately you know that I'm big into QTP. What's QTP? Glad you asked. QTP means simply Question the Premise. Have an idea? Ask yourself why do I believe that. You will (like I have) find out that a lot of what you believe is based on false assumptions. Again, much like my assumption on organ donation.

Be open to new experiences. Seek out new experiences and expose yourself to different cultures, people, and ideas. Where I live in Midwest North America, there are many people who have never been out of our state, let alone out of the country. One of the greatest experiences in my life was eating a bowl of soup with a chicken's foot hanging out of it while deep in South America in the ministry. Was it good, you might ask? Honestly, I don't remember. Because while I was grossing out over a chicken foot in my soup was exactly the moment when my interpreter leaned over and whispered into my ear: "This family has worked for a month to be able to buy that chicken. They consider it an honor to host you, so please eat it or you will offend them."

I had to get rid of a wrong perspective and think divergently about chicken-foot soup. Spoiler alert! The soup didn't kill me and evidently was good because I do remember finishing it. I'm glad that I thought about it divergently on a different level than I was accustomed to. So, surround yourself with diverse people. Being around people with diverse backgrounds, experiences, and perspectives can help you think more divergently.

Play with the possibilities. Imagine different scenarios and consider what the outcomes might be. Be open minded and be willing to consider new and unconventional ideas.

When you're stuck on a problem, take a break, and do something completely different. This can help you come back to the problem with fresh eyes and new perspectives.

Explore new things. Trying new activities, reading new books, and traveling to new places can help you think in fresh and different ways. Play and have fun. Cindy (who comes from an education background) has taught me that while kids are playing games, doing puzzles, or solving riddles they can be learning at the same time. Even babies should have sensory toys that develop their minds. Use fun to try to generate some new ideas.

Try writing. One last idea to help you along with your divergent thinking is journaling. Writing down your thoughts and ideas will help you explore different aspects of a problem or challenge. Plus, in a year when you look back, you'll say something like, "Wow, I remember when I was going through that." Hopefully you will have learned a lot of good things since then and can continue to remember that things are going to be ok today. It's just another challenge or problem to solve.

"The quality of your thinking determines the quality of your life." – A.R. Bernard

Chapter 5

Our Need for Community

This past year I took the last half of December off because I decided it had been a really taxing year for me. In February I had released *The Hero Within* which hit bestseller, then we did the audiobook, and things were good in my life.

Out of disaster came Craig Version 2.0 like a phoenix out of the fire, and I was off to tell everyone in the world about the lives of organ transplants. The first of December came, and I was trying to get this book to my editor. Several things came out of nowhere including the hospitalization of my pops. I went back and reread chapter two on embracing uncertainty. It was suddenly certain that I was having to live out what I was writing. Things went on pause, and I took the rest of the month off.

During that time, I did a lot of QTP-ing. I "questioned the premise" of everything including why I was writing this book. It was during this time I took several personality tests. I find it funny that most people that see me think I'm a really outgoing people person, when in all actuality I'm not. I took both tests, and their assessments proved to be very accurate. (If you are interested in this, email me and I'll share.)

Both tests confirmed what I had pretty much already known: that I am more content being with my loved ones and close friends in an intimate setting than being crowd oriented. That's kind of funny coming from someone who has spoken to about 15,000 people in one meeting alone and yet finds more joy being with only a few.

It can start small

During the pandemic some people were in bliss to be alone for a while, and yet that same isolation put others in a very volatile place. Even as sick as I was during all this, waiting for an organ match and battling severe cognitive function problems due to the ammonia in my system, I longed for people.

I would take the time every week just to sit on my porch and talk with my new friend who took care of my yard (from about 15 feet away). I would be like a kid in the candy store every Thursday, because I knew Don was coming to mow my yard. Every week I would muster enough energy to get to a rocker on the porch and just talk for five minutes. To me those five minutes were everything; it was a lifeline of hope.

I don't think my friend Don will ever know how much those five minutes every week meant to me! He had shown true empathy, and it helped me hold on until I got the call that they had found a match for my transplant.

How many Dons have come across your path during your times of need? More importantly how many people have you come in contact with and perhaps been a Don to those people? There is a huge difference between having followers and likes on social media versus having a true friend! So many people will take comfort in having a large number of followers on social media. Would they hold your hand while you're on death's doorstep? I don't think so. To become a better human now, we must understand our need (and others' need) for community.

If it hadn't been for people caring, I have concluded that I might not have made it. For some, all they had to share with me was their care and empathy, and it was life-giving! Sometimes it's more than enough just to know someone is standing with you. Again, it is life-giving!

I'm sure there were days when Don didn't have the time or the patience to listen to this half-crazed ammonia brain person on the porch. Let's face it, people are inconvenient! If you want respect instead of likes on social media, start showing up for your people! Be there when it's inconvenient for you. Be that better human!

Start with those closest to you. I admitted earlier in this book that I basically stunk when those close to me had problems. I had that "I've got problems of my own" attitude. My problems were things like I had to work late, look what the kids did now, my car insurance went up etc. My problems were not things of importance, rather they were inconveniences. Since my Craig Version 2.0 inciting incident, I have noticed so many around me that are hurting in one of their three parts (mind, body, heart). It's as if a veil had been lifted from my eyes.

People wet from the storms of life are all around you. You must get your eyes off yourself. Then and only then will you see them all in your life space. When you start reaching out to them, you will often find the answers to your own problems showing up while you are helping them. It's a beautiful thing!

Your community reflects on you

Let's talk about community and what I know now as an extremely important topic. Community is basically a group of people typically sharing the same social values. People long for the acceptance of community, and social media tried to fill the gap. It tried to monopolize on the need for community, and it's a good thing if used correctly.

Why do we as humans have to clarify all the time what is good and bad, and why do we keep running from what is bad to something new? Why does every generation think their music is the best? All these things are shaped by social opinions that your mind takes in on a daily basis from your community.

Do you remember when we talked about your mind being a human computer and that putting bad data in causes bad output? It definitely applies here. What social groups you receive input from will shape your life. It doesn't matter if it's in person or via a form of social media, it still affects us the same.

I believe it was Jim Rohn that said that you are the average of the top five people you hang out with. I guess my parents were correct all the times they said to me, "You are judged by the people you run with!" I guess that I just didn't really understand what they were telling me, which is that society will lump you in with and then view you as the group you run with. In all honesty my communities weren't good and my high school years were tumultuous to say the least for my parents.

They also always used to tell me, "One bad apple ruins the whole basket." Another lecture about my friends is how I saw it then. Now I realize that as in many things they were correct. It does matter who you run with! Even worse, society will classify you with the people you run with.

I'm not nearly as worried about society's opinions as I am about what's good for me and what I'm mentally digesting from those around me. This is not to say that your reputation is not important. It's just that everything starts with what you're influenced by.

The benefits of community

So how is community good for us, you might ask. Let's take a look at some of the benefits to see just why community is so important to us. Remember earlier when I talked about the assessment test that I took? One of the things that became very clear was that I'm a learner. That is my nature, and when I've learned what I need and feel that I've mastered it to some extent that's when I move on to the next topic of need or interest.

This is also why I find it so important to hang around people who will challenge my strengths. In this type of setting, I can receive from them while giving to others in the same group. To be clear, you must not be only receiving in a community but also be equally as giving. This might not be the case at first. You will of course need time to acquaint yourself and get to where you feel comfortable to share.

I heard it somewhere and have lived by it since: "You should always leave more than you take." On podcasts that I've been on that's been my goal. It wasn't so much as to promote my books as it was to help build their audience, and in turn my audience grows too! We should always be receiving and giving in any community. That's what makes it healthy.

On the phone one day, I was talking to someone who had read the first book and they were telling me how much they enjoyed it. As I ended the call, I thanked her for her support and told her that I had a Zoom meeting coming up in a few minutes. Much to my surprise she exclaimed, "You mean with the Liver Tribe? I think that is so cool!"

That in itself amazed me that she had remembered that from the book, yet alone that she saw the importance of it. As I responded with a hearty yes, I dug a little deeper and found out that there was a longing in her to have that same type of relationships. I love my Tribe! We now just call it Tribe because we also have multi-visceral transplants in the group too.

"As iron sharpens iron, so one person sharpens another." Solomon said this, and he was one of the wisest men on the earth at the time. My divergent mind says that this adage would probably work the same in a negative connotation! As a bad apple makes other bad apples, so one dull and blunt person can create others. It's pretty simple: "Sharp makes sharp!" It matters who you hang with!

Many have asked me what goes on in a Tribe meeting. There is the usual "who is up next" type of thing with people supporting those that are getting ready for transplant. Then we usually talk about what's normal and not normal after the operation. It can contain all kinds of frank and sometimes "yucky" stuff like how to clean a surgery drain tube etc.

It is an amazingly supportive group, and I consider them as loved ones. But with that said, if it ever turned into a gripe and complain group, I would protect myself and leave. It sounds harsh, but negativity breads negativity, and that's as far away from empathy and miracles as you can get.

Wise old Solomon also said this:

Two are better than one,

because they have a good return for their labor:

If either of them falls down,

Craig W. Huber

one can help the other up.

But pity anyone who falls

and has no one to help them up.

Also, if two lie down together, they will keep warm.

But how can one keep warm alone?

Though one may be overpowered,

two can defend themselves.

A cord of three strands is not quickly broken.[1]

It would seem from what he said that we get stronger by the number of people we keep with us. This would be a good first test if you're considering a community to align yourself with. I will say that this takes time to develop; it is NOT instantaneous! You and your new "peeps" need time to build a trust factor and then develop it into a tight community.

If the community ceases to grow, it will become a club. You must always be able to both receive and give to gain the benefits that you and others need from a community. When a community becomes a club, all will become the same, and anyone who comes in must conform to that image. A lot of evil has also come from clubs in the form of being supremist. Whether by religion, race, or even our sexuality we should never be divisive.

We are for Team Better Human! We have not yet attained it but are continually striving along the side of like-minded individuals willing to grow and change for the better.

Beware of any group with a zero-tolerance attitude. In person or online you need to find your tribe!

In addition to my first Tribe, I also have a tribe of writers that I hang with. In my writer's tribe there are people who have had a lot of success, some who have not, and even some who have just started. I love that group too! The common elements it shares with the first Tribe are growth and caring. It is a place I can bare my soul and frustrations and of course my victories! It is a place I can receive knowledge while passing on the knowledge I have.

Over the years I have found out that most men avoid deep relationships. This is probably from a bunch of bad data that was dumped in there like "Real men don't cry," and other idiotic ideas. Yes, I realize that sounds harsh. My guess is, though, that you've never been with one of these men when they finally do crack open. It's not a pretty sight.

Over the past year, there have been multiple headlines that modern men are having some deep relational problems. It wasn't the pandemic that did this. That just squeezed out what was already inside: all that bad data that was put in there a long time ago that their minds keep trying to make sense of.

This is why I think we have such a surge in life coaches, therapists, and online counseling services. Some of us were given a lot of bad advice earlier in our life and it has caused a lot of problems later in our life. It is just bad data, so strive to erase, replace, and move on! Put the new data in and you will produce new results! This is where community comes in;

they help you back up on your feet, dust you off, and then point you in the right direction. I cannot emphatically tell you enough that you need community!

Divergent thinking in a community

Since we established that practice makes perfect, here are some ways you can practice divergent thinking when dealing with other people, both within and outside of your community. You can use these in a private or a group setting.

These practices will improve your communication skills. You should notice that communication and community come from the same Latin phrase. They definitely not only rely on each other but are entwined throughout.

First, practice active listening. Listen to others and to try to understand their perspectives. This can always help you see things from different angles and generate new ideas. This is where we get the phrase "Get a new set of eyes on it." Be open minded to these new ideas and perspectives, even if they are different from your own.

Asking open ended questions that encourage others to share their thoughts and ideas helps build community. Of course, we need to always encourage not only collaboration but also trial and error. Not every idea you've had has worked out, so why not let others also work their way through some things. Collaboration can bring different perspectives, skills, and experiences that can lead to more creative outcomes for the community.

Finally, always value diversity in your community. Different perspectives, cultures, and backgrounds can bring rich new ideas and solutions that you would have never come up with.

Now I know that many of you already acknowledge these things, but it's time to master them! As I've heard it said many times, "If you are the smartest person in the room, then you are in the wrong room."

Chapter 6

Being Present vs. Living in the
Moment

Throughout this book I have included a vast amount of the lessons I've learned since my life-saving transplant surgery. But out of everything we've covered in the previous chapters, this chapter has been, is, and probably will be something I will always be actively working on for the entirety of my life!

As an author, I of course would love that you take all the lessons in this book and apply them. As a fellow human, I realize only a small percent of folks actually change their actions after hearing a new truth that would truly help them if they would only apply it.

Most of the time I think if we hear someone speak or perhaps read their books, we can become very stirred and motivated. That's great! Motivation is fabulous; however, it is never enough. You must practice this new truth to the point where you're living it, not just parroting it to others. It all goes back to the old saying, "You can talk the talk, but can you walk the walk?"

For me this was definitely one of the more pronounced areas where I was failing, and worse yet, few noticed. **I always showed up! But rarely was I present and, even worse, I hardly ever experienced living in the moment!**

You might be the same way with your loved ones and friends. You might make the baseball or football games, the birthday parties, and maybe the occasional romantic night out. You showed up for sure. You were there, and that's what matters, right?

Well, that's what I thought. . .until I found out:

I was wrong. Not partially but completely and fully wrong.

This is probably why writing this chapter has taken so long. I wanted to make sure that I had it right and could commit to living it out.

Do you remember the story about the spinning dog and its cage? When I discovered about being present and living in the moment, it truly changed me from the inside out and now keeps me from all that spinning. Remember, you were made to frolic not spin, so let's get going. Let's do this!

The practice of being present

When I started researching about being present and living in the moment, I found that most people assume that both are referring to the same practice. But is that true? Being present and living in the moment are indeed similar concepts. Both involve you being fully aware and mindful of the moment and not just showing up for the event.

In my case, I guess I had reached that point in my life where I felt that simply giving of my time was enough. What I ultimately have learned is that you can definitely show up to an occasion, but that doesn't mean you are present. It takes practice.

To push the point a little more, the word practice is defined as "the actual application or use of an idea, belief, or method, as opposed to theories related to it." You can sit inside and talk about cutting the grass a million different ways, but until you actually do the work your yard is just going to look terrible.

So, back to the practice of being present. As I've said before, first we show up. Easy first step for all of us, and one you might have already done today when you went to work. You simply showed up. Good job! However, your boss might like a little more from you than you just showing up. They might perhaps like to see your value to them by you doing your work.

This goes for your loved ones too! They don't want you to just show up! They want your value to them: your love, caring, and even listening skills. To them (your boss and loved ones), it was never about you simply showing up for the event. It was about whether you were actually present and giving of yourself.

A stranger's real-life example

The best way for me to explain what being present means is by showing you what it's not. A while back, Cindy and I went out for a quiet romantic dinner. We often like to get a booth, someplace off to the side where we can relax and have a nice dinner with some "riveting" conversation about our day. Sometimes while dining out, I will glance around to see what other diners are having and to see if they're enjoying their dining experience.

That evening I spotted a young couple holding hands, staring into each other's eyes, lost in love. I politely pointed them out to Cindy while making a remark about how cute they looked. That same evening another younger couple was sitting not too far from our table. They also caught my eye, and I waited for the fireworks of love to start exploding between them. Perhaps I was looking for a repeat of that "magical young love" moment.

Instead, when I looked up at their table, they both were staring down. At first, I didn't know what to think. Perhaps they were praying and giving thanks for their food. I wasn't sure. It just seemed odd that they both were staring at their laps while on a date in a nice restaurant.

Then it hit me! I realized they each were texting or on social media on the phones in their laps. I laughed and poked Cindy saying, "Do you think they are talking to each other via text?" It was funny at the moment, until it wasn't anymore.

Throughout the evening my eyes would wander around the room, and several times I spotted that young couple again. Not much had improved. I sat there wondering who was responsible for the distance between them. As we exited the restaurant that night, I remember myself making a crack about that young couple and the evils of modern technology and social media. I missed the point entirely.

It mattered not whose fault it was that they didn't connect. What does matter is that they appeared not even to try! They showed up, but did they get anything out of the dinner? Did they grow closer or discover something new about each other? I don't know for sure, but I expect not.

I'm NOT saying that every moment you have with another human is going to be this momentous event. I AM saying, though, that it takes more than you just showing up. It takes effort and sometimes hard work. It's not easy when you're wiped out, brain dead, and completely exhausted from your work and then a loved one or a close friend needs you. YUCK! Defiantly not what you signed up for. Can't they see that you've already given your all?

The choice is no one's but yours. Are you just going to show up? Or are you going to not only show up but be present too? It's all up to you; it's your decision.

What's your time zone?

Here's a good rule of thumb that I use on being present. *Being present refers to the state of being fully engaged in and attentive to the current moment, rather than being preoccupied with the past or future.*

You get to decide which time zone you are going to live in: past, present, or future. That's all you get to choose from, and you can only use one at a time. So, choose wisely in the moment, knowing that showing up and being preoccupied is NOT the same as being present!

What time zone do you mostly dwell in when you're with others? Does your mind wander off to the future or perhaps to past things or events? We don't listen well when we're preoccupied in another time zone. Were you thinking about the past? How things went wacky at work hours ago or even later than that? Or perhaps were you thinking of all the things that you should be doing, and all things that you have to absolutely get done later. If so, then you were in the future and were not being present.

It is **not** wrong for those thoughts to come into your head while you are trying to be present. I do believe however that those thoughts (if you dwell on them) will NOT serve you well on your journey to be present in the moment!

So, to be present is to simply chose the correct time zone that you want your mind to dwell in! Haven't you ever been out with a friend who keeps recounting some trauma in their life over and over rather than listening to what you wanted to talk with them about?

I know that I have, and at times I just wanted to scream "Get over it!" This was my reaction to them not wanting to join in relationship with me but instead dwell on a problem that we've already talked about a million times before. They were stuck in the past and not being present.

Just do you

Now before you run out to set the world straight, let me stop you and tell you one very, very important thing. You are only responsible for yourself to be present! Don't worry about whether everyone around you is present or not. That's not your job. Your job is to be a better human now. Trust me, it will be contagious.

I believe you will find that as you become present, others will notice and naturally join in. It might not be on the first time or even a couple of times after that. Try to remember that they are probably not going to recognize the new "present" you at first. They likely have gotten used to you just showing up, or maybe you've all been just showing up together.

It doesn't matter one way or the other. Again, please just do you! You be the driving force; you be the spark that starts the fire. Don't wait for even your partner to be present. Just start trying to be in the present for yourself:

1. Show up.
2. Become present: chose your time zone!
3. Live in the moment.

Living in the moment cannot happen until you've become present. To my knowledge it cannot be an independent action nor practiced apart from being present.

Manage your moments

Another good way to describe living in the moment is as if you were a great movie director. You walk on to the set, see it in total, and begin to think about the really important scenes ahead and what you want to convey to your audience.

If you want to get really imaginative, try picturing yourself holding your hands up just like a director framing their picture in front of them. They do this to mimic what something would look like through the lens of a camera and to figure out how to show the details of the story. What do you notice in the moment as you look through your hands?

To live in the moment is to recognize and highlight in your own mind the importance of the often unnoticed but very important parts of a scene in your life. For instance:

"I'm sitting at my desk, it's early morning, and the sun is peaking in through the blinds. I can hear the birds singing especially this morning; even the doves are cooing. The steam is coming off my cup of freshly brewed coffee, the smell wafts through the room, and then I taste my favorite blend . . . mmm, dark and stormy with just a touch of raw sugar. Next, my cat Mango enters the room, meowing a good morning."

This all happened in a moment. In a blink of an eye so much is going on around you. Are you noticing everything and everyone around you?

Your life really is nothing but a series of connected moments! Talk about time management. Manage your moments!

Because often before you can say "Cut!" as the director, your movie stops, every moment is past, and the credits roll.

This might seem dark to you but hear me out on this, please. If you keep letting the moments go by unrecognized, you will never enjoy the scenes in your life or, worse yet, you could sleep through what everyone else considered an epic movie.

What makes an epic movie? All kinds of different scenes: some happy, some sad, but all are part of the story! It's the same in our lives. If you want a full life, you must monitor your moments. When the difficult scenes come up, we want to avoid them. Instead, lean into them, experience them, and revel in all that life has given you in the moment.

I did not say you would always enjoy this process. I'm just asking you to not only show up and be present but also to embrace the moment. It is just that, and it will pass and then be only a memory. The film will end, and the credits will roll.

As I said at the beginning of the chapter, this has been the toughest area of growth for me in becoming a better human. I always showed up! But only sometimes was I present, and barely did I live in the moment.

My real-life example

Before I give you some concrete ideas on how to practice all this, let me tell you about an unpleasant scene in my life when I would not normally have been present, nor would I have lived in the moment that day. I would have shown up, but instead of practicing being present and living in the moment I would have become numb and avoided the tough scene. I would keep face, but I typically would just let it all bleed together into a big blur that I called life.

I get a sick sort of feeling deep inside me when I think about all those times when I wasn't being present or living in the moment, and how disappointing it would have been if my movie had ended and the credits rolled without me having given it my all. When it's over I don't want to be remembered for a poor performance. I am everyday trying to give the performance of my life now!

This scene in my life happened over a couple of horrendous days. If you're a pet lover, you will understand in a deeper way than perhaps if you've never had a pet. Up to a couple of months ago we had two cats, Lilly and Mango. One day we noticed Lilly was not drinking or eating like normal, and we just figured she might have had a cold, etc. It had happened before with her eyes and nose, and she would get (as we call it) "goopy eyes."

Unfortunately, things got worse, and Cindy was at work when Lilly started losing control of her bladder. It was horrible. You could see the shame in her eyes, and it was clear that things weren't going well. I called Cindy, she called the vet, and we took her in. The vet said she was getting older, and her vitals were good. Blood work was done, and she received several shots including an antibiotic and vitamins. We left feeling somewhat hopeful and with a couple of prescriptions.

For this chapter, I thought about sharing everything we went through during those days. Instead, let me just say that things went from bad to worse, and we had to put Lilly down. We had been down this road once before, and it was then that I gave a poor performance. With Lilly, I was determined to not only show up but to also be present and in the moment. To me, it was one of the toughest things I had faced since almost losing my life.

Previously when we had to put a pet down, I just declared that it was Cindy's and that I just couldn't go with her. And then I probably just numbed out and waited for another day hoping it wouldn't be as bad. Cindy had to ask her friend to go with her instead of her spouse, and I realize now how sad of a scene it was.

Not in this current scene! Never again was I going to check out. I was going to be present for Cindy and Lilly and, not only that, I was going to face things straight on. The night before we would take Lilly to the vet, I even had the thought that perhaps I would take an anti-anxiety medication (doctor prescribed) to make it through the day. It would not have been wrong of me in any way to take the medication so I could be there one hundred percent. I'm not going to lie and say how strong I was. I was a mess!! I carried the anti-anxiety meds with me in my pocket as an emergency parachute.

It was a truly horrible time, and the night before was filled with Lilly having ungodly seizures. I was there; I was present. And more importantly, as bad as it was, I was with her all the way through. I was fully alive that day when I looked into those big, beautiful eyes and said goodbye—and it hurt like hell!

It hurt even worse when I found out that she had passed due to liver failure! I felt so much that day and still do today as I write this to you. I can see her eyes as if she was begging me for help, and I could do nothing to help her. I cried for days, and I'm crying like a baby as I write this. I miss her.

It was that day that I learned to be present in a different way. I was real with myself and those I love. It was a scene that makes me sad, but it's also a scene that makes me proud that I did it.

I showed up.

I was present.

I lived in the moment, and I remember it.

Ways to practice being present

Being present with people means being fully aware of how you're connecting with another person. It's not just physically being in the same place with someone. It's willingly giving them your undivided attention.

Living in the moment means you pay attention to your present experiences instead of letting your mind get caught up in stressful and upsetting thoughts. It means letting go of the past and not waiting for the future. It means living your life consciously, aware that each moment you breathe is a gift. Being present and engaged leads you into living in the moment.

Here are some ideas on ways to be more present with people:

- Use your phone less (including social media).

- Give your undivided attention to those you are with.
- Bring your mind back when it wanders.
- Use a meal or tasks (like a walk) to ease difficult conversations.
- Identify when your mind wanders off.
- Don't rely on rehearsed stories in your head. (It might not go like that, anyway.)
- Be genuinely curious about what the other person has to say.
- Ask questions.
- Avoid making assumptions or filling in the rest of their sentence. (Note to self . . .)
- Listen attentively, noticing facial expressions, body language, and other nonverbal cues.
- Don't tune out while they're talking.
- Don't deny their experiences or talk down.
- Don't just tell them to focus on the positive.
- Don't change the topic.
- Ask the person to tell you more. Take the time to dig deeper.
- Try to be like a mirror and reflect back, in a caring way, the most important points you are hearing. Others will be reassured, and you can keep yourself in check.

It can be hard to live in the moment when the following things cause you to check out of the present:

- Having a wandering mind
- Too many distractions

- Feeling overwhelmed
- Reality being too painful
- Constant distractions
- Feelings of anxiety and stress
- Viewing time as a continuous and linear process (one blur)
- Dwelling in the past or worrying about the future
- Living in the past trying to solve an unsolvable problem
- Constantly talking to ourselves in a negative or unhealthy way

Living in the moment every day will take practice and effort. Here are a few ways that may help you:

1. **Practice mindfulness.** Mindfulness is the practice of being present and aware of one's thoughts, feelings, and surroundings. Mindfulness exercises such as meditation, yoga, and deep breathing can help you focus on the present moment.

2. **Avoid distractions.** Distractions such as social media, television, and constant notifications can pull you away from the present moment. Limiting the time spent on these activities can help you focus on the present.

3. **Engage in activities that require your focus.** Activities such as puzzles, games, gardening, cooking, journaling, and art can help you focus on the task at hand and be present in the moment.

4. **Take a break from technology.**
   Disconnecting from technology from time to time
   will help you be able to focus on your surroundings
   and be present in the moment.
5. **Appreciate the small things.** Taking time to
   appreciate the small things in life such as the
   beauty of nature, a delicious meal, or doing a kind
   act can help you focus on the present. When was
   the last time you had a moment of pure joy?
6. **Be grateful.** Reflecting on what you are grateful
   for in the present moment can shift your focus and
   help you appreciate your current situation.

It's important to remember that it's not always possible to live in the present moment all the time—and it's normal to get caught up in the past or worry about the future—but you don't have to live there! With some practice and effort, it's more than possible to live in the moment more often than not.

As for me, I also find it's not possible to live in the present every moment, every minute, every day. However, with patience and practice I'm going to show up, be present, and live in the moment as often as I can.

Hopefully, when my credits roll, they'll show I was a better human than when I started!

You got this!

Chapter 7

The Power of Thankfulness and Gratitude

W hen I started to write this book, I wanted to create something of value. Something that others could read and perhaps and save themselves a lot of heartache and pain. Every chapter has covered something that I've strived toward since the inciting incident of my transplant surgery.

You could almost say that every chapter was born out of a struggle. Whether it was internal or external, they all came about from the labor of what I call "internal friction." This is when *you* have to work on *you*! Often, people mistakenly equate this feeling to a restlessness or even maybe feeling a little irritated with "everything and everyone." That, my friend, is your alarm going off inside of you declaring that it's time to work on you!

During this growth and discovery journey I have seen so many different sides of me that had been lurking but never really blossomed. As I said in the last chapter, I want us to be fully bloomed and at our best when the final credits roll. We must stay present in this day and hopeful for tomorrow!

So, if you have a "grumpy" side to you get ready for some internal friction and, more importantly, a lasting change.

Positivity vs. gratitude

Before my liver decided it had been through enough and was in the process of checking out, I had been up for a promotion that I had worked on for several years. I planned my approach and had a good business strategy to take my team to another level and break all the new sales goals. Everyone thought I would be given the position for sure. I felt confident.

The interview went well (at least to my expectations), and I left feeling pretty good about the probability of getting the new job. I had, however, noticed that I didn't connect like I wanted to with the interviewer. When talking to another person who had applied, it came up that they had just gone into the meeting and sat and BS'd with the interviewer. I thought about how strange of a business decision it was to just BS your way through the meeting. Then the news came.

I had been turned down for the job. I was shocked to say the least. The final blow came when I was told that "I wasn't positive enough for the position." Several of my team came to me saying things like, "How could they say that you weren't positive? You're the most positive person I've ever met!" I too was stumped. How could I not have been positive with a business plan that was proven to work? All I was doing was being realistic. Did that mean I wasn't positive?

I could have written this chapter and called it "The Power of Positivity." Instead, I named it "The Power of Thankfulness and Gratitude." Mostly this was due to the fact that we've all run into that one really overly positive person. You know—the type of positivity that causes them to basically ignore and deny what is really happening all around them as they just smile and glaze over. They try to live on hype which does not sustain. Perhaps that was why I didn't get the job; I just wasn't hyped enough.

It started me thinking, "Why have people considered me a positive person?" In my pre-transplant life, I was always considered positive. But was I?

As I mentioned earlier, I had taken a strengths test to see myself from another perspective. Ironically, out of 34 strengths listed my positivity came in at a whopping 25. There were 24 other things that I was stronger at. To narrow it down for you even more, you should only concentrate mostly on your top ten strengths. Positivity was at 24 out of 34. Quite the distance from my top ten strengths that are common to me!

So why do people consider me positive? I seem to be even more like that since the surgery, and yet I didn't get the position because I was being too realistic. Why am I perceived as both positive and not positive at the same time?

Then it hit me. People mistook my thankfulness and gratitude for positivity!

Thankful FOR everything or IN everything?

It is against my nature to encourage hype. It is, however, very much my nature to be thankful and full of gratitude. As I said before, it is even more so now being a transplant survivor. Way back in the day when I was in the ministry, I often taught about being thankful and the power of thanksgiving.

Interestingly enough, it seemed like every time I would teach on this, we would get reports back of miracles happening. It wasn't due to my teaching style or strength. It was clearly due to people regaining their thankfulness and gratitude. In turn that leads to hope which is the predecessor to faith.

Let's think about it in an earthly way. I am a proud father, yet all my children at one time or another have acted like idiots. I know; shocking, right? Who do you want to do things for? The disrespectful, rude, and ungrateful or the ones that thank you for everything you've done for them. Jesus often equated our heavenly Father with our earthly fathers. We are loved so much more than even our earthly fathers have the capabilities of! Smile, you are loved. Be thankful and have gratitude for it might just be the key to unlock what you seek.

Someday I would like to write a book called *The Church Did What?* We have twisted scriptures for centuries. Don't believe me? I often hear people say that we need to be thankful for everything. "Well, just be thankful for that . . . just stay positive!" Sorry, but that just hurts a lot of people and defeats them even before they get into the depths of their problem. It is not a truth, and if you think that is what's in the scriptures you are incorrect. Let's look at the verse everyone interprets rather than taking it literally.

"In everything give thanks; for this is the will of God for you in Christ Jesus"[1] is what the apostle told the church of the Thessalonians.

Did you catch that? You are to give thanks IN everything, not FOR everything. What would you think of your kids if they came to you and thanked you FOR the kids picking on them on the bus? What would you think of your child thanking you FOR the neighbor's dog biting them?

That's crazy, Craig, I would never allow that! Well, of course, and you are an earthly parent.

We are to be thankful IN all things not FOR all things. The apostles had both good and bad times in their lives, and they were trying to instill in the early church an attitude of thankfulness and gratitude. I'm sure you've realized by now that life in general is a series of events tied together. So, whether they're good or bad circumstances, be thankful IN them not FOR them, and just see what happens.

I asked Google's Generative AI "Is there a religion or belief system that opposes thankfulness?" and got exactly the reply I thought I would:

"It doesn't look like there's a religion or belief system that opposes thankfulness. In fact, religious traditions including Judaism, Christianity, Islam, Buddhism, and Hinduism all encourage cultivating gratitude as an important moral virtue."

Now I realize that some of you are study bugs, and some are not. So, to you study bugs this is a good jumping off point for you to go and research. The rest of us are going just to take it simply and boldly. We ARE to be thankful and have gratitude at ALL times and IN all things because we know He cares for us!

Practicing thankfulness and gratitude

In every chapter I've tried to leave you with some ideas to practice. So how do you be thankful and have gratitude? We first know that it's not a fake pretentious positivity, and worse yet it does not seem to be natural to us as humans. I believe we were born with both hands outstretched and in need of a parent. We were perhaps thankful for the little things when we were kids, but as we grew older, we became more cynical and more grumbly.

When we went to the store when I was a kid, sometimes when you were really good, you'd get to buy a gumball out of the machine when leaving. Typically, it was a penny or perhaps a nickel in cost. I remember being fascinated with the quarter machine because it had prizes in little bubble containers. It might have been a spider ring or rub off tattoos or even a simple rubber ball that would bounce "thousands" of feet! The capsule that it came in was just as cool as the toy, sometimes.

Now as an adult you might walk across the grocery parking lot and kick one of those capsules while grumbling about those "@#$*!" littering kids! What changed? In short, you lost the magic of appreciating the small things. Somehow over the years many of us got caught up in life and lost the art of being thankful. We became like that poor dog in the first chapter, always spinning when we were made to frolic! This leads us to the first thing we need to realize about the power of thankfulness and gratitude.

In general, thankfulness and gratitude are NOT natural for us at this point if we haven't been practicing them. Like I said earlier, we were probably born with the ability to be grateful, but our attention was drawn away and we became like a bratty kid that expects everything and feels entitled. Again, if you were the parent and all your kid did was grumble and ask for more things, how would you feel? Would you want to give that child more?

We are more than likely to give more to the child that is thankful and connected to us than to the spoiled child who continually wants more and even asks for things that aren't conducive to their life. Practice being childlike. Find joy in the things around you. This does not just happen. You must create it. You are responsible for your own happiness. Sorry, I wish we could blame it on all the crazy people that cause turmoil in our life, but you truly are the captain of your own vessel when it comes to happiness.

We must put ourselves in a state of thankfulness and grati-tude. Remember the chapter on divergent thinking? Well, this is where you are going to have to think on a new level. Celebrate everything from this point forward. The little things, the big things, the easy and the hard things—find the joy and the thankfulness in all of it, and you will find your way through that problem you're facing. Stir it up on the inside of you, and let it seep out and infect those around you. Thankfulness and gratitude might just be the key to unlocking your miracle.

Putting it all together:

- It doesn't come naturally.
- You have to practice it before it becomes your nature again.
- The cares and fears of this world oppose thankfulness and gratitude. Just like the time zones in the last chapter, we get to choose between borrowing trouble and getting caught up in the cares of life versus practicing thankfulness and gratitude.
- Go on a gratitude walk and start listing all the things you can be grateful for as you walk.
- My planner has a daily space for "three things I'm grateful for." Do the same in yours or start a gratitude journal.
- While you are at it, write down something every day that you are looking forward to.
- Make thankfulness and gratitude a part of (I vote for the majority of) your prayers and meditation (quiet-time thinking).
- Use your power of remembrance. What you remember you tend to dwell on, and what you dwell on is usually where you'll end up. You can't drive down the road without running into a ditch while concentrating only on your rearview mirror. You must look ahead – focus on where you are

going to end up, not where you've been, and please, please don't put it in park!

As they say, practice makes perfect, but they left out that it's also sometimes the hardest part! Please join me on this journey of thankfulness and gratitude. I am so thankful for you and that you took your precious time to listen to me about the importance of these life lessons that I've learned since my transplant. I am forever grateful.

Chapter 8

About Hindsight

"The real trick in life is to turn hindsight into foresight that reveals insight." ~ Robin Sharma
"After the event, even a fool is wise." ~ Homer

Someone said hindsight is 20/20, and it does seem true for most of the time. In *The Hero Within* I talk about life after my transplant when I wrestled with the questions, and I quote:

"Who (Who am I now?), What (What comes next?), and Why (Why me and not someone else?)" is still something I struggle with; perhaps I always will. Maybe I just shouldn't have gotten so caught up in what I thought life was all about before my organ transplant."

Now in hindsight I realize that I cannot live in the past nor the future. I live in the now. I plan for the future; I just don't put my trust in it. **Depression comes from the regret of the past. Anxiety comes from fear of the**

future! Paraphrasing Shakespeare, "A hero dies once . . . but a coward dies 1,000 times." It will never serve you to live in the past or the future. We can glance into the past to learn while peering into the future for hope. The reality again is we can only operate in the now!

You only have one life to live, so why not make it your best life? No matter what you're facing, there is always another step! It has been an amazing two years of life since my surgery. There have been some really hard places with a few easy ones along the way. To say it has been a journey would be an understatement; at times it was hair-raising. Here's the thing though, I made it and so will you. It might not come out exactly like you want it to, but you will go on.

Hopefully somewhere in the thick of things you will find yourself and realize that you weren't nearly as lost as you thought you were! Some of us need to learn to give ourselves some grace. In hindsight, at times I have probably have been my worst enemy. There is and always will be that temptation to beat myself up over and over for something I can't undo. So, what do we have left? Just now. The question really is what are you going to do with it?

Remember the funny movie *Groundhog Day* with Bill Murray? He keeps waking up to the alarm clock everyday— but it's the same day he keeps living over and over. At first it seems to be a nightmare, then he realizes he can affect his life and others' lives by getting better at his own existence. He does this by practicing day after (the same) day. His only goal was to get better, and it wasn't easy for him.

And it is the same with us. It's not going to be easy, and somedays it will seem like the day may never end. We hold the keys to what can change our lives, and it is up to us to make them what we want. We are kind of like the character Bill Murray played in the movie because we just keep trying. His changes affected so many people, and in the end, he saw the value of his life. If you haven't seen the movie, go look it up. There's a great message hidden in a lot of silliness.

As I review everything we've covered, I find myself wondering whether for some people it might seem overwhelming to change while for others it might seem trite or even simple. How much you want to work on being a better human is determined only by you.

It's as if we are running a relay race together, each of us having our own race within the greater race of the team. I am, however, now handing you the baton. Go run your race and give it your all because there is someone waiting on you for the next hand-off!

This book is called ***A Better Human Now***. It is <u>not</u> called *A Prefect Human Now* because there are none to be found. Every day I wake up and determine to be a better human. Even if it's only better by one percent, after a year I figure I'll be 365 percent better than I was. If I only hit the 25 percent mark, I am still better than if I had never tried.

Today I am going to be a better human now. I sincerely hope you'll join me!

Craig

. . .

Didn't get to read about the "inciting incident"? Here's where you can read how it all started: "The Hero Within"

I really appreciate all of your feedback, and I love hearing what you have to say.
I need your input to make the next version of this book and my future books better.
Please leave me an honest review on Amazon or wherever you bought the book, and know that I'm truly grateful for your taking the time to do this.
Thanks so much!
Craig W. Huber – craig@huberbooks.com

About the Author

Craig Huber has an entrepreneurial spirit. He has owned his own business, founded a 501c3 nonprofit organization, and was in the ministry for about two decades. During that time, he travelled extensively in North, Central, and South America. He also has a background in sales and sales management. When he's not writing, you'll find him enjoying family, all things culinary, and occasionally fishing. He and Cindy enjoy traveling most of all and doing what the locals do. You can find them in the mountains, lakes, and oceans or even swimming with sharks and rays larger than themselves. Every day is a new journey since receiving a new lease on life.

Can You Help?

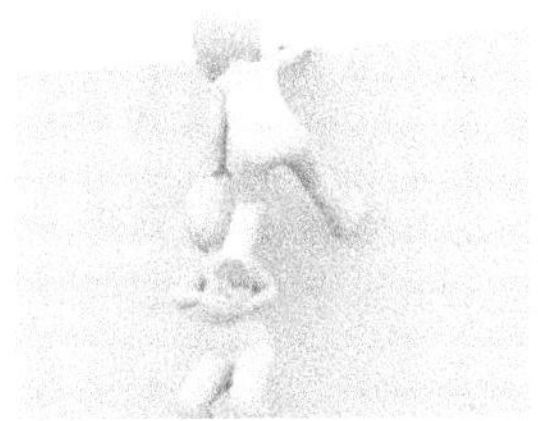

Thank You for Reading My Book!
I really appreciate all of your feedback, and I love hearing
what you have to say.
I need your input to make the next version of this book and
my future books better.
Please leave me an honest review on Amazon or wherever
you bought the book, and know that I'm truly grateful for
your taking the time to do this.
Thanks so much!
Craig W. Huber – craig@huberbooks.com

Endnotes

2. Embracing Uncertainty

1. Matt. 5:45 (New American Standard Version)

3. Empathy, Miracles, and Changing Internally

1. John 8:4-5 (New American Standard Version)
2. John 8:8-9 (New American Standard Version)
3. John 8:10-11 (New American Standard Version)

5. Our Need for Community

1. Eccles. 4:9-12 (New International Version)

7. The Power of Thankfulness and Gratitude

1. 1 Thess. 5:18 (New American Standard Version)